VOTING

A TRUE BOOK
by
Sarah De Capua

Φ

Children's Press®
A Division of Scholastic Inc.

New York Toronto London Auckland Sydney
Mexico City New Delhi Hong Kong
Danbury, Connecticut

A person registering to vote

Reading Consultant
Nanci R. Vargus, Ed.D.
*Teacher in Residence
University of Indianapolis
Indianapolis, Indiana*

*Author's Dedication:
To Rebecca*

*The photograph on the cover
shows a person voting. The
photograph on the title page
shows a voter placing her
marked ballot in a ballot box.*

Library of Congress Cataloging-in-Publication Data

De Capua, Sarah.
    Voting / by Sarah De Capua.
        p.   cm. — (A True book)
    Includes bibliographical references and index.
    ISBN 0-516-22330-5 (lib. bdg.)   0-516-27365-5 (pbk.)
    1. Voting—United States—Juvenile literature. 2. Elections—United
States—Juvenile literature. [1. Voting. 2. Elections.] I. Title. II. Series.
JK1978 .D42 2002
324.6'5'0973—dc21   00-048308

Contents

Schoolchildren preparing
for a classroom election

What Is Voting?

Is there about to be an election in your classroom or school? Perhaps the adults you know are learning about local or national candidates so they can decide whom to vote for.

Voting is an important part of contributing to a community. People vote to choose their

Voters gather to greet a candidate.

leaders. The person who gets the most votes is the winner.

Mayors, town-council members, governors, and the president of the United States are among the many government leaders who are voted into office. In some elections, people also vote on issues, such as whether a highway should be built through their town.

People voting

The ancient Greeks were among the first people to vote. More than 2,500 years ago they began voting to choose public officials, or leaders. Usually they voted by raising their hands.

About 2,000 years ago, the Romans began using the secret ballot. With a secret ballot, people vote in private. Then they put their ballot in a container with other marked ballots. People don't have to worry about what other people might think of their choice.

In ancient Rome, the members of the Roman senate were elected by the people through a secret ballot.

From about 4 B.C. to the A.D. 1700s, kings and queens ruled most of the world's countries. The word of a king or queen was law. Ordinary people had no chance to vote for leaders.

They had no control over their laws or how their government was run.

By the late 1700s, people in many countries began to rebel, or fight against their leaders. American colonists rebelled against Great Britain's government. That rebellion turned into the American Revolutionary War (1775–83).

When the colonies became the United States of America, the people wanted their new country to be a democracy.

The word *democracy* means "government by the people." In a democracy, the people choose their government leaders through elections.

The members of the Constitutional Convention of 1787 agreed that in the United States, government leaders would be elected by the people.

Women (above), American Indians (right), and black Americans (below) were among those who had to struggle to win the right to vote in the United States.

By voting for leaders who represent their views, people have a voice in how their government is run.

However, at that time, not everyone in the United States was given such a voice. Only white men who owned land were allowed to vote. Poor people, black Americans, women, and American Indians were not allowed to vote. Over the next 200 years, though, each group gained the legal right to vote.

Who Can Vote?

Today, any American-born or naturalized citizen of the United States who is at least eighteen years old is eligible to vote in local, state, and national elections. A naturalized citizen is someone who was born in another country, moved to the United States

14

These voters are all at least eighteen years old.

to live permanently, and later became a U.S. citizen.

Every state requires that a person must live in that state for a certain period of time before he or she can vote. The time period is usually about one month. Some states allow new residents to vote right away in elections for president and vice president. This is because these are national offices that affect people throughout the United States.

Before being permitted to vote, people must register to vote. They must fill out a voter-registration form with their name, address, age, and the

People registering to vote

length of time they have lived
in an area. In some states,
people are also asked to
choose which political party
they support. In the United
States, the two major political

North Carolina Department
Motor Vehicles

VOTER REGISTRATION
HERE

VOTER REGISTRATION

A government worker
explaining voter registration
to a new voter

parties are the Republican
Party and the Democratic
Party. If a voter doesn't wish

to support one of these two parties, he or she can register as an independent.

This information is kept in the voter's town hall or city hall in an office called the registrar (REH-juh-strahr) of voters. The registrar of voters keeps a list of all the people in the area who are eligible to vote. Before a person can vote, his or her name must appear on the list of registered voters.

How Votes Are Cast

On Election Day, registered voters report to a building called a polling place. Schools, stores, churches, or other buildings are often used as polling places. A private home may also serve as a polling place.

A voter first reports to a clerk and gives his or her name or

address. The clerk finds the voter's name on the voter-registration list. The voter shows the clerk identification, and the clerk checks off the voter's name. Sometimes a voter is

An election worker helps a voter sign in.

asked to sign his or her name. The voter is now ready to vote.

Different kinds of voting equipment are used in different areas. For example, many places use a punchcard-ballot system. Voters are given a ballot card.

Then they step into a voting booth, where the ballot can be marked in private. In the booth, they place the card flat against a clipboard-sized device. They use a tool called a stylus to poke a

This voter is using a stylus on a punch-card ballot (below). This is a punchcard ballot after it has been marked (right).

hole next to the candidate or issue they want to vote for. After voting, voters either place their ballot in a locked ballot box or feed it into a computer. The computer then records the vote.

A voter puts her marked ballot in a ballot box.

Marksense ballots are cards
with issues and candidates'
names printed on them. Next to
each name or issue is an empty
rectangle, circle, or oval. Voters
use a pencil to color in the
empty space beside the person

or issue they are voting for. A computer later records the dark marks on the ballots as votes. Lottery tickets and school standardized tests work the same way as marksense ballots.

Voting machines are another method of voting. After being checked in by a clerk, the voter steps up to the machine. The voter pulls a large lever that closes a curtain behind him or her. The names of all the candidates are listed in front of the voter. A small lever is above

each name. The voter pulls down the levers above the names of the candidates he or she supports. When voting is complete, the voter pulls on the large lever again to open the curtain. At that time, the votes are recorded in the machine. The voting machine is then ready for the next voter.

A touch-screen DRE

Direct recording electronic systems, or DREs, are the newest way to cast votes. They are computerized versions of voting machines. Voters use a touch-screen or push-buttons to record their votes. The votes are stored inside the machines on a cartridge or diskette.

In a few places, paper ballots are still used. With these, voters simply write an X or other mark next to the names of their chosen candidates.

A voter marking a paper ballot

On Election Day, polling places stay open for many hours so that everyone has a chance to vote.

Voting takes place throughout Election Day. Some polling places are open from 6 A.M. until 10 or 11 P.M. Voting hours are long so that everyone in a community has a chance to vote.

How Votes Are Counted

When polling places close, an important part of Election Day takes place—counting the votes. Voters watch television or listen to the radio to find out the results of the election.

In polling places where paper ballots were used, clerks open the ballot boxes.

Election workers
counting paper ballots

The clerks count the votes by
hand. Depending on how
many votes must be counted,
it may take several hours to
determine the winner.

It is faster and easier to
count the votes from polling

places where voting machines are used. It takes only a few minutes for clerks to unlock each voting machine and copy the vote totals from its record. Punchcard, mark-sense, and DRE ballots can also be counted quickly since their results are tallied by computer.

When clerks at each polling place have finished counting the votes, the results are announced to the public. This

is usually done through television, radio, and newspaper
reporters. It is also possible
to find out the results of an
election on the Internet.

National elections involve voting for the next president and vice president. In these elections, millions of votes must be counted. Often, the winner is not announced until late at night. Many voters may not find out who the winner is until the following morning.

Another way in which national elections are different is the way in which the winner is determined. In the United States, citizens do not vote

After the voting results are in, winning candidates make acceptance speeches. Here, President Bill Clinton makes his acceptance speech after being reelected in 1996.

directly for the president. They really cast their votes for electors pledged to a certain candidate.

Each state has a specific number of electors, from 3 to 54,

depending on the state's population. States with more people have more electors. Usually, the candidate who wins the most citizens' votes in each state receives all the state's electors', or electoral, votes. These electors cast the actual votes for the president. There are a total of 538 electoral votes. A presidential candidate needs at least 270 electoral votes to win the election.

Too Close To Call

When the 2000 presidential election was held, it took 36 days to find out who won! The two major candidates were Republican George W. Bush and Democrat Al Gore. After the voting ended on November 7, the race was too close to call. Florida was the deciding state. Whoever won Florida's 25 electoral votes would win the presidency. But the

race was so close in Florida that the votes were recounted several times.

People argued over whether the election process in Florida had been fair. Some Florida voters thought the ballots were confusing. Others thought they had mistakenly voted for the wrong candidate. With the punchcard ballots used in some areas, recount officials argued about which votes should count and which should not.

For weeks, the nation waited while thousands of Florida votes were recounted. Lawyers for both candidates argued in court about the recounts. On

Democratic and Republican recount officials examining Florida punchcard ballots

December 13, the U.S. Supreme Court stopped the counting. George W. Bush won Florida—and the election—by only 537 votes.

The events in Florida made many Americans want easier, more accurate ways of placing and counting votes.

Why You Should Vote

Why should you learn about voting
and politics now if you can't vote
until you are eighteen? Because
voting is an important part of living
in a democracy. People can help
change their communities for the
better by supporting leaders who
have good solutions to important
issues. Even though you can't vote

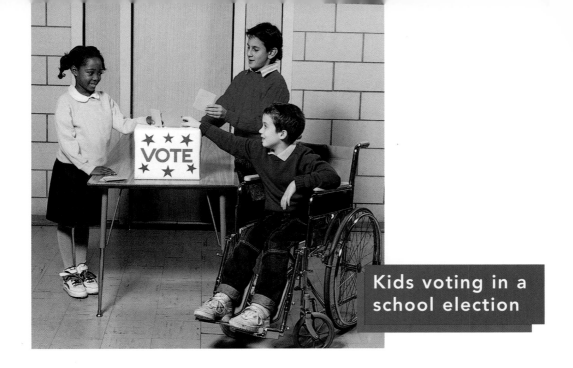

yet, you can still write to elected officials. You can tell them what you think they should do about issues that concern you.

Also, you don't have to wait until you're eighteen to become involved in classroom and school-wide elections. What do you think

of the candidates? How do they want to solve problems? Do you trust them to keep their promises? Ask them questions so you will be well informed when it is time for you to vote.

There are ways you can get involved in local, state, and national elections too. Volunteer to put up posters in your neighborhood for your favorite candidate. Dedicated volunteers are always needed at a candidate's campaign headquarters. You can stuff envelopes, make copies, or run errands. Perhaps you will enjoy your involvement so much that you will run for office yourself someday. People may be voting for you!

You can show your support for a political candidate long before you are old enough to vote.

To Find Out More

Here are some additional resources to help you learn more about voting and elections:

 **Books**

De Capua, Sarah. **Becoming a Citizen.** Children's Press, 2002.

De Capua, Sarah. **Running for Public Office.** Children's Press, 2002.

Gutman, Dan. **Landslide! A Kid's Guide to the U.S. Elections.** Aladdin, 2000

Hewitt, Sally. **The Romans.** Children's Press, 1995.

Scher, Linda. **The Vote: Making Your Voice Heard.** Raintree Steck-Vaughn, 1996.

Organizations and Online Sites

DemocracyNet

http://www.democracynet .org

Enter your zip code to find out who's running for offices in your town and where they stand on important issues.

Federal Election Commission

999 E Street NW
Washington, DC 20463
http://www.fec.gov

This government agency enforces election laws and oversees public funding of presidential elections.

Politics1

http://www.politics1.com

Provides links to all political parties and elections in the United States. Also provides information on political debates and a gallery of historic campaign buttons.

Project Vote Smart

http://www.vote-smart.org

This site was selected by the American Political Science Association as the "Best Political Web Site." It provides information about government and how it works, as well as data on the positions and voting records of politicians.

45

Important Words

accurate free from mistakes

ballot card or piece of paper on which a person's vote is recorded

candidate person who is running in an election

citizenship the rights, duties, and privileges that come with living in a certain place

clerk person who keeps records

contributing being a part of

election act or process of choosing someone or deciding something by voting

polling place place where people vote

register to sign up

requirement something that you need to do or to have in order to do something else

46

Index

Meet the Author

Sarah De Capua received her master of arts in teaching in 1993 and has since been educating children, first as a teacher and currently as an editor and author of children's books. Other books she has written for Children's Press include: *Paying Taxes, Running for Public Office, and Serving on a Jury* (True Books); *J.C. Watts, Jr.: Character Counts* (Community Builders); and several titles in the Rookie-Read-About® geography series.

Ms. De Capua resides in Colorado.